CRACKING EGGS

UNIVERSITY OF CENTRAL FLORIDA PRESS

Contemporary Poetry Series

ORLANDO

CRACKING EGGS

POEMS BY

Katherine Soniat

Library of Congress Cataloging-in-Publication Data

Soniat, Katherine.
  Cracking eggs: poems / by Katherine Soniat.
    p.   cm. — (Contemporary poetry series)
    ISBN 0-8130-0973-1 (alk. paper). — ISBN 0-8130-0992-8 (pbk.:
  alk. paper)
    I. Title. II. Series: Contemporary poetry series (Orlando, Fla.)
  PS3569.065396C7   1990
  811'.54—dc20   89-20387
                                                        CIP

University Presses of Florida is the central agency for scholarly publishing of the State of Florida's university system, producing books selected for publication by the faculty editorial committees of Florida's nine public universities. Orders for books published by all member presses should be addressed to University Presses of Florida, 15 NW 15th Street, Gainesville, Florida 32603.

Acknowledgments

Many thanks to the editors of the magazines in which these poems appeared:

Anthology of Magazine Verse and Yearbook of American Poetry: "Cameos," "Four O'Clocks"
Artemis: "The Radio Says Buy," "Recitations for the Girls' School"
Carolina Quarterly: "Picturing the Landscape"
Chowder Review: "Cameos"
The Christian Science Monitor: "Screen Porch"
College English: "Short Street"
The Fiddlehead: "Opening Passages"
Images: "Summer Tomatoes"
The Ohio Journal: "Evolution in the South Bronx"
The Kansas Quarterly: "Sawdust," "Luster's Gate"
The Louisville Review: "Three-Year-Old Applauding Mushrooms after Rain"
The Malahat Review: "Rabbit, Looking for Home"
Memphis State Review: "#2 Yellow Wooden Pencil: 1953"
The Michigan Quarterly: "Drawing in Boundaries"
The Mississippi Valley Review: "Dragon's Tooth Ridge"
Modern Poetry Studies: "Breath on the Mirror"
Mss.: "Cages"
The Music of What Happens (poetry anthology): "Something Left to Say"
The Nation: "Still Life with Grass, Fur, and Air"
New Letters: "Winter Toys"
The New Virginia Review: "Summer Tea"
The North American Review: "That Far from Home," "October"

Northeast: "The Cloakroom," "Late Exchanges"
The Pacific Review: "Eating Soap"
Poet and Critic: "Myrtle Tree"
The Prairie Schooner: "15th-Century Flat"
Poetry: "Lighthouse Telephone"
The Smith: "Four-O'Clocks"
The South Florida Poetry Review: "A Place by the Window"
The Southern Review: "Rembrandt's Vanities"
The Southwest Review: "An Ending" (published as "Nightwatch"),
     "Palm Sunday Race"
Spoon River Quarterly: "Smile"
Tar River Poetry Review: "Standing Wet and Close"
Threepenny Review: "Strange Music"
Yarrow: "Roadtrip"
Yankee: "Cracking Eggs"

Some of these poems were first published in a chapbook, *Winter Toys*, published by Green Tower Press, Maryville, Missouri.

Contents

One

Cameos

When the train moves off,
I watch its headlight circle,
a cool white finger gliding
from spruce to spruce. Bit
by bit, it picks out and lights
a world: a hawk roosting its life
away on little more than air,
and the skull of last year's fox
nailed to a tree.

Sometimes, it all comes clear,
the moon pouring vivid branches
through each window. Why
can't every moment crack open
like those trees so full of revelation
when the train wanders at midnight?

I see the train light pause
and take one snowy skull,
saying this is it. Then
it moves on, saying the same,
over and over, the same.

Lighthouse Telephone

You held your hands to my face
when I was four
and blistering with sun, that broken
boat sputtering finally toward home.
You made a breeze with them,
said they were palm trees
near my window, miles ago, in Key West.

Key West had slipped so easily
away, the salt-spray sun
sinking down in orange, twilight
drifting upon us in a fishing boat
that would not start. The only sound
was waves slapping
the boatside in the wind.

Then the lighthouse came alive,
like one match struck in the dark
and blown out, then another.
You tied a hatchet to your
scarlet bathing suit in the starlight,
and swam away. The whole Gulf
swam up to me, floating alone.

The sun rose pale from the water
as I bobbed blocks or miles from you
and that white bone of a lighthouse.
Dozing. Waking. Sleeping.
All around the Gulf was
endless,
the sun growing high again and yellow.

Until the sky began to drone, and a seaplane
floated out of a cloud. My head
was blister-hot, the sun was spinning
gold, voices swam over me from men

in white uniforms: someone in red
had been swimming in a shallows
of sharks. The day froze

to dead calm. *Luck* was all
I heard one say, as your hand
appeared at the seaplane door.
The boat rocked like a cradle,
my skin went cool with noon.
On a green tide of sharks and luck,
we rode all the way home.

Roadtrip

In Tinsaw County, north Alabama,
there was season to count on,
never far from the roadtrips

in the one-horse wagon
or those in the two-tone Ford

heading south to the next aunt's
parlor-chintz, Coke bottles,
iced green, bucketed beneath the dash,

their glassy bottoms embossed
with one unremarkable town after another.

We rolled our cheeks with bottle-chill,
rattling our way past Flomaton
and down the dusty hours
to the coast,

the road map blowing on the front seat,
our carload headed into the paths
of red clay and scrub-oak hum.

A Slow Take

Roadway sealed in crystal,
my car skidding on ice—
                    and those crowlike
boulders had always seemed so comforting,
half-feathered in snowy white,
each a little fable with an ending
that should not hurt.
                    But snow never was
a coat for pleasure, even at its liquid best:
swimmers gasp sideways for breath,
eyeing a horizon awash with space,
all that loss summering beneath.
                    And so today
the snow's adrift with implication—
each boulder skidding past as a possible
stop on this slip down an ice
sheet, this sheet a shroud,
                    the picture swimming,
incomprehensible as trying to grasp
moments on ice, or swap slick fables
with the air.

Opening Passages

Even as children we took hints
of later storms
whispered off as heat by nursery fans.
Our throats went dry at the thought.

Later, words began to open
every day. They stole volume
from the wind-thoughts.
When the rains began

we heard it all from beneath
the shape our lives took on.
We heard hammers quickly building
on the far side of the lake

where room upon silent room
lit up, mindful
of nursery wind. The rains.

Myrtle Tree

It is human in spring to want
to begin. To begin in time,
time depends on who is looking
at it, and today, Sister, I am
seeing time through you:

                                 it is July
as I set off down a muddy path,
a voice calling through the myrtle tree
sister, sister, you've got a new sister.
A lizard stops in the fence vine
to puff his throat. He is wary,
slow to move, and I stand
featuring myself close to my mother
on the bed, the fan creaking that whole
month of June while she sweated and did not
move so you could be born.

                             You will
never remember this. This was when time
had no before, before the world was set
in motion by a voice in the myrtle tree.

Luster's Gate

On the backroad our car floats
the curves like a top, headlights
throwing warning polish on the hills
that pour us down the valley and
swing us into the dip called Luster's Gate
where the barn collie's teeth flash
with his chain. It's as if we could
never stop. And wouldn't.

The grace is swift the rabbit
moves by. He leaps forward
to take the road, then startles
in the headlights—little Charon,
suddenly seeing the other side.

At daylight, roads narrow in the country
while on the sky life spreads
in starts and stops. Starlings
flood the air, then turn
and sprinkle darkly backwards
as if a finger beckoned an all clear
then slammed its hand up
like a brake to the heart.

Something Left to Say

for my mother (1918–1972)

That night I was not there,
and for moments somehow you returned
from weeks of nothing
but wanderings in your head.
They said you opened your eyes,
knew the room well.
I knew my absence well—
how I could not stand by breathing
in that sick-dark room
while you settled deeper
in the four-poster
under its canopy of roses.

Now, at every window,
through white summer hats,
through candlelight shining in my hair,
voices whisper *stay*. Outside
the mockingbird goes on
with his frail-throated song.
Your final words are repeated
like a sharp wind that's never left
my back. They told me how you called
my name, looked around. And looked.

Intermezzo

Here floats the schooner, the cape
of green water you thought perfect.
The pier stands solid underfoot,
the running lights of boats
glowing red or green. The evening
passes, correctly cool.
Behind you, the shore sounds
with women's laughter and iced drinks in glass.
Soon a tune lifts from the violins.
This is a world you dream of.

But not the one as you dreamed it.
The dream where you see the running lights
and step easily out toward the pier's end
until suddenly you are at the edge,
the rail changing to cobweb,
a thousand feet of wind gusting under
you, over a schooner anchored far below
on the sea. The sea is reduced,
taken down. You are looking straight
down. The pier that seemed so sure
has little to do with you—
more with this fat man shoving your stomach
into the webby rail, the schooner drifting
dizzily below. You break from his hands,
make for the gay laughter, perhaps
part of another dream you could enter
midway. You find yourself in a hotel
lobby painted too many shades of rose and jade

and the violins have settled into
drum as you turn up in The Women's Room
where two women speak of solid
white houses, beefsteaks and cars.
Steadily, they nod. The drums beat
louder and you picture the schooner

changing to a dark weight swaying on ropes,
moving deeper into the ground

when suddenly this little intermezzo
of drums and grave talk halts.
A black woman in a turban appears,
whispering through your hair
that this is Eluria,
miles into Africa. Drumming
washes through you like waves
closing above your head
a thousand feet below in the sea.

The Cloakroom

Mostly now she forgets
but for alleys and damp afternoons—
then, she's there again,
daylight falling behind her
like a salmon swimming downstream,
him looming like a bear,
the smell of rainy wool closing in:

the janitor's older son
fondles braids,
his breath matching, touching
the pulses in her neck
as his hands move down on her,
down slowly past her throat.
Squeezing a damp sweater sleeve,
she holds her life apart—
the heavy smell of coastlines
and far away, him rising
through a fog, breathing
on some stranger's body's edge.

Sometimes she thinks
it's all a tale she heard,
this bear holding a small, pink fish.
But in the rainy tunnels of afternoon
she is part of this, off in a corner,
watching, building scales around herself.

Summer Tea

At first, the shape was a thing—
a blowing bag? hat in the field?
Then she saw the whining coon,
her dogs tossing him like an old
summer doll. Once she had pictured

fear like this—it gloomed windows,
hung in the imaginary trees
making cat-whines as she sat
arranging her dollhouse, its tiny
folk for August tea.

Now that cry was coming clear,
swift as the knowledge of waking
alone and knowing *alone* is the first
and final private thing. The coon's
whine came clear and she came

with a leash, thrashing two dogs
and a coon, not knowing
just what was being saved, the four
of them swirling before something
brisk and unquestioning on the other side.

Later, she returned to that coon,
dog-crippled, now undergoing men
with their shovel as he hunched
to the ground as if to pull it
up for privacy, one of them

mumbling *rabies* and *go on, hit him.*
You afraid? The man beat slowly.
And the coon's whine slowed
to that windy sound outside
a dollhouse.

Two

While We Speak

The air's a shrivel of morning skunk
and sunshine gives everything a hot,
dry licking. If I stoop any closer,
this half-eaten rabbit will let me know
if it is liver or intestines,
shiny and sexual, that the lithe cat licks.

*

From under the lilac, the blacksnake
uncurls to sun. I rinse him
up and down with the hose,
cold sending him fading like a genie
through the house crack, taken
in by the domestic dark of mice.

*

Twilight, and the white horse
scratches his neck on the rickety gate,
making it creak. The dog growls
at each of his peaceful, ruminating
giant's hooves, evening cooling
crisp as a carrot.

*

Darkness coats the wild sweet pea
while a whippoorwill swings in
closer now from his daily hideout.
His call vibrates with afterthought:
the all-hands-on-deck
when not one weathered voice replies.

Winter Toys

Winter, and my father
steamed his gray destroyer straight for Cyprus,
deep into what they called the Cold War,

and in his wake gifts arrived—
a gold charm of a gondola from Venice,
a peasant marionette from Genoa—

while in Sunday school, I watched
the wall map unfold with the cedars of Lebanon,
the Mediterranean blue under the galleys

of ancient sailing men. Full-moon nights,
my mother would pull down photos
of the USS *South Dakota*, that battleship

she used as memory: "There, on the deck,
that's you in a christening dress," she would smile
and be far away from me on those nights.

I lived inside the gestures and red enamel
smile of my lady marionette. She danced
her own string quartet, two arms, two legs

flying in time to *Genoa, Genoa*. With a shake
of my bracelet charms, I imagined a rocking gondola
making headway in a world I thought

Jesus would love to take long, watery walks in,
while somewhere to the east, my father in dress whites
wandered lost in evergreens—all of us feeling

lost, as my marionette tapped
her toes, nodding *yes*
to any stretch of the imagination.

Skins

1. Makeup

At four I believed I could live
forever in a fifth-floor turret room—
either I would be the fairy or live
in a fairy tale. And always I would stand out.

Today in the parking lot of the Econolodge
shattered red sunglasses stand out, bright
as blood on a railroad track. They are red
as *The Red Shoes*, that movie where the beautiful,

powdered ballerina jumped from love to her
train-track death. "Dance Ballerina Dance" was the song
I heard over and over behind the closed door,
a rhythm men wooed my mother to.

All of it sheer invention.

2. Off-color

14 ROOMS FOR RENT reads the sign,
and out of the brownstone flies a Chinese woman
shouting after a man with his garbage pail
but do you really, I mean really like black persons?
He shoves his trash down the storm sewer,
and she's tugging at his sleeve with *they strangest.*

Across the street, at the side entrance
to the museum, two men pose in stone.
The older stoops, clinging to the younger:
The Prodigal Returns. They clasp,
and the woman keeps imploring,
wanting this man just to look up
from his pail of eggshells and toast.

3. Fiberglass

I want to touch them—
these two naked men and a woman,
recast a century beyond

their source: "Déjeuner sur L'herbe."
Three-dimensional now in this museum,
all three bared to fiberglass flesh,

wiglets curled for genitals and skulls.
Each leans toward the spread of dark
wine and bread—form suggesting

essence on earth: man, woman
fruit and grain come together
in a stone house.

4. Albino

At dawn above the fire escape,
an albino squirrel veers
out of reality, twirls

down the tree next to Sadie's
All Knighter, pickled eggs
and pigfeet briny in the window.

Then he scampers away
from the jars of salty sunlight
as if he understood the price on palest flesh.

5.

The horse lies flat
in an empty lot, February
sun spread on his hide.

Death-animal or hoodwinked drowse
of false spring?

Now the two dead ears
twitch. He's listening
to the dirt throb.

Lessons

for Shelton

On Sundays I would hold your hand
to the summer screen, airy with colors,

hummingbirds beak-deep in fuschia.
I said *hummingbird* with your finger

to my lips, then hummed a rosy
lullaby as we walked out to touch

each crisp little landscape,
starting slow with the hedge.

We picked a wooden basket of dandelions,
blew the sky into stars of thistles.

You huffed like my giant busy at creation.
Now the day is no longer a spray of dandelions

or hummingbirds perfectly suspended,
and only I recall how I grew

dandelions and hummingbirds
with your fingers to my mouth.

Cages

We wander the Washington Zoo,
each wrapped in our own winter.
In the Monkey House, the great ape
draws us to his own set of tears—
he keeps jostling his mate with supplication
and leathered paws. Lumbering off, she eats
nuggets, and he moves in again, then out
until placing his huge sad monkey head
on the wall, he stands still.

Outside, in a cage of earth and sun,
the Giant Panda, mateless,
beats his heart out on a pie pan,
directing himself with a wand of bamboo.

Drawing in Boundaries

Strange, how we feared the Indians
as they circled us in 3-D,
and now the flatness of our lives

threatens behind our own closed doors.
We camp on distant throw rugs,
installed at intervals

in each other's lives.
Sending signals, we settle
without benefit of sky

or words, those whispers
securing the dark
of a circled wagon train.

Breath on the Mirror

The world is always shaping
new hollows, smoothing old ones,
and we go on trying to fit ourselves
to one another. Little was said
when we lay there, our bodies close.
So many days, that was how we started,
in a room that held space for daybreak
and the few late stars.

But I rose, and it was not
from dream. Wrapping myself in woolens,
I wished you a long, slow sleep.
I wished the clocks would stop,
the birds fall silent in the leaves.
Moving from room to room, I turned
each photograph flat, placed a close
warm breath on every mirror
until I made myself and all
the background disappear.

Late Exchanges

A year, and we recover
words that lack memory,
that mean what we see. You watch
closely the cat, as she loops her paws
at the air. We string sentences made
of the weather, of plants, their need
for water.

I look down at my hands,
your hands, and wonder what it was
that passed between them. Once
it was you and I, quiet, watching
something almost like this evening
disappear. In that silence
the cat flicked her paw unnoticed.

Now we push words to pinpoint
the moment of late light.
The cat's gestures, the green leaves
and spigot water—all the tiny elements
enlarge. This watering can, tipped
in my hand, swells with an ocean
that separates: all that distance,
and this water angling through sunlight
between us.

An Ending

Windows offer little hope tonight—
the stars are falling,
lighting old tides and river willows
in my head as I breathe on,
torn by the presence of a dead
and a dreamed-of mother:
mother-of-all-the-long-nights,
we spent ourselves, our daylights,
waiting for high tide to end your kneel
at the river's edge . . .

but I know this tale of vigils,
building myself into levee fires,
scanning the shore with light.
Nightly, my arms reached for you,
water rising in the willow trees.

Four-O'Clocks

The sleep of late afternoon
is an undertow, pulling
me to struggle with twilight
as a child. This is a glass dream:
mirrors full of me rise
and fall, lit by a single
candle flame. Eyes flicker
in the speckled age of looking glass,
staring toward a music box
dying midway through a nursery rhyme.

Glass child, child with my eyes,
you're still breathing the threat
of evening in the heavy smell
of four-o'clocks. I'm caught
face down, held to the solitary
lengths of afternoon. Dried thoughts
rearrange themselves, unfold
on the wet cheeks of a child,
left at dusk like a scattering
of wild flowers.

Cloudy Logic

Because the gray cat died
on the convent's grotto to the Virgin,
I decided the nuns laid poison
out for my purring web named Cloudy.
I shoveled her a grave under Mary's hand
near the dwarf azalea, confusing death
with the acid soil: so the world's the place,
so lovely, we come upon to die. Therefore,
I thought it must be the earth set out
that kills us. I could almost feel
the ground shake, people stamping
their feet at gray clouds above their grottoes.
I stamped mine hard over my dead cat.

Smile

From the grass embankment
you wave me off with your flashlight,
away from your knowledge of death.
Like a ghost lit with direction,
you are on the way out this cold season
and it's a hard coal I swallow back,

remembering back to your beginning—
when I was seven I came upon you
as, perhaps, the strangest man ever.
But that November the light was candlelight.
You were the stepfather, I, the flower girl,
and my mother, an unimaginable bride.
I descended our house stairs, clutching
pale carnations past each rosy-lipped
aunt whispering hard *smile, smile.*

I had arrived, a memory at the wedding,
my mother's small appendage from another
life. There we stood, woven into three
before a mantelpiece of candles. Later
that night the bedlamp burned all night
after the two of you left—the hallway,
the stairwell, the front porch growing
quieter, then quiet. I sank into her
old four-poster bed, dreaming red
lips twisting the word *smile.*

But that was years before
what you know now in the dark
as you turn away from my presence,
the lit phantom of a November night.

A Place by the Window

It's that simple. Simple
as this time of year when so little
stays. A year since you went away
and the days went on doing their trick
of silk scarves, making bright
explosions with the fall leaves,
then disappearing in a tumble
over the hillside—the year
gone. Tonight I see clear through
the year laid down with you inside.
I'm trying to see you thinned
to a fly wing, a dust
I can be done with. But memory

fiddles backwards through the stones,
making what should not,
come to light. And there it is:
the chair you brought to the window.
Not that you wanted to include
the flowers and trees. You saw
yourself slipping away,
and there I was like a slow, breathing
army trailing you to the edge.
You found your place by the window,
and looked away.

Three

That Far from Home

I

If it only depended on the young
circus elephant, swaying by the river
eating kudzu, or
the reeling paddle wheeler

chirping off "Summertime,"
then you could barely help
remembering. Memory would arrive
like a basket of creations

dropped into your lap
just before the evening lamps went out—
each little item that old,
that far from home:

the half-grown circus pet
turned out to pasture
with nothing to remember, nothing
to commend him to the future

or the past. Only four, large-nailed
gray feet on which to balance
and make a life of it. You recall
the thick tent, the cold and rainy hay.

II

With the paddle wheeler singing
you can almost catch a glimpse
of the bride boarding
for her Mississippi wedding trip,

the whistle calling
out to the folk of coastal

towns clustered in the willows.
They came out to watch

the summer shade pour through
the lyric of a *daddy-rich-
and-a-momma-good-looking.*
But the music stops on the paddle wheeler,

and your small basket of circus tents
and riverboats melts into the past,
into a river twining through the trees,
quivering with light.

III

Like that day the door cracked open
with sunlight before you headed out,
walking straight into memory.
Going out after something to remember,

you left the house standing
solidly behind you, only the river
rushing on to lead you
on beneath the trees—

a slim river shouldering roots
you would never see
to believe in,
like hands that glide at windows

on All Hallows' Eve
when so many are out looking
and so much is held in—a time
when memory and the season

swing into one
to nudge open the doorway

lined with sunlight,
the sounds of water pouring through.

You moved past that door, that house
to feel at home collecting
for a basket, things frail
and hidden as the river.

Barncoming

Strange to a mountain home,
we sit with Christmas
while the cat hisses at the snow,

offering it an imperious look.
The fire hisses dampness into smoke,
and I leave for a walk, breathing

deeply a deepening freeze, wind
stripping the abandoned house up the road,
its one ax heaved into the last

piece of wood, as if someone had drawn
in his breath and decided to suddenly
forget where he lived, leaving only

the Chinese kite tethered to make swipes
at the coming-down white weather.
A lit barn glows in a field,

and the neighbor's slow cows alone
seem easy with recall
as they ponder the way back.

Rabbit, Looking for Home

Once he owned my backyard,
and more: my black Persian cat.
Her furriness enticed him
to recall a thickly rabbited earth.
He lusted after cats, any cats,
declared himself a cat to prowl

the world at large. And there
he held a Siamese at bay on a car engine
in range of Sunday bells and patent leather
shoes tapping down the street.
Cat or rabbit, it made no difference,
his heart thumping, his world
turned upside down. He crouched
like a domestic dream gone bad,
not a field or hawk in sight.

All this just to press down,
pelt to soft pelt,
and believe in a cane field again—
where no Chevrolet holds
furred illusion high
on an engine, origin Detroit.

Recitation for the Girls' School

Once it was Evangeline from her forest
primeval who complicated things. We

had her prelude to recite, brimming
with *oaks like Druids whose hoary*

beards of moss fell to their bosoms.
One after another we stammered into

that ripe forest laced with "bosoms"
and "whores." Those words we choked back

advanced in scarlet silks on windy street
corners in our minds while Miss Norwood,

straightening, kept saying *yes, yes,*
young lady, please do go on with it.

And indeed we did go on, our whole
eighth grade of girls was delivered

in four years to the plight of Hester Prynne.
But we were free young women behind the walls

of that girls' school, thick and stone gray.
We were reading racy stuff under the rays

of the Eisenhower smile
as Headmistress caught a worldview

filtering through her bay window
in the form of naked Greeks: two new

marble statues affixed to a neighbor's
two brick chimney tops, their bodies gently

curved in memory of being maids and men.
Headmistress took due note, ordered

those nude statues to dismount,
and as the chimneys retracted

such a classic arrangement, we flipped
the last page on Hester Prynne.

Topic: Methods of Courtship

I said consider what it is no longer—
no longer the maiden in the pantry
waiting to unlace her bodice, hoping
this is the way out past the barn
and up the hillpath to beyond.
                              But later,
reading through the sleepy essays of my
eight-o'clock males, I see how
they've proceeded to write that old
tale of prey:
                    poor male, poor animal,
hugged to death as usual by the female
of his choice, that ancient ring of damsels
waving their arms, each signaling
distress in a singularly old way.
                              In the midst
of these ink-dark essays, there arises
Joel's, the poet of the class, enthralled
with the future of his words: *I will
persuade myself to her brown eyes
under a shade tree, and if she does not go
for the brilliance of my mind, there's still
the fiery ruby necklace to go with the Mercedes,
sunroofed, and some flowers . . .*
                              Oh, heady stuff,
oh where's the one exemplary lady who will
prove his case, I think as the pollen flies.
But can I say this in red to a young man
lost in the brilliance of his shade tree?

Dragon's Tooth Ridge

An old tale glints from the stars,
while we dash off history out of confusion.

See the Bear rise in his sparkled night-fur?
Stars, quiet animals of the dark, wait,

their beginnings once as tempestuous as ours
below on the grass and berry-colored earth.

Tonight, the heavens loom with ancestry—
that long line back through constellations

to star-burst, each pattern kindled
from blue heat of the past.

15th-Century Flat

Probably it was no more
than an abbess sprinkling chants
above the crippled girl
that brought her to a leap
of the imagination. But miracles
want to be raised and pinned
to the proper century
with credit given the villager
who rose in sunlight. Walked.

For every cripple named inside
a shaft of light, there is no accounting
for the girl, any girl,
who for one moment attaches
her broken knees to flashing intuition,
and like a child watching water
turn clear, bottomless as summer tea,
she lifts and comes up with all
her limbs in motion. Moves.

There was no church bell,
no promised place in history. Perhaps
it *was* near Florence on a Wednesday,
but there was little indication of anything
except summer as the abbess turned
to clipping roses, the girl walking
like measurement through the tall grass.

#2 Yellow Wooden Pencil: 1953

A line of men watches
the first receive a name
for the darkness they live
inside: *colored* or *black*.
On the metal table not one
yellow pencil rolls in the sunny
wind, the African veldt rolling
on all sides, wheatlike
but without wheat.

The man in the glossy shoes
reaches up, sticks one pencil
into a tall man's hair,
whose head, then body, bend
and hang. The moment hangs.
If that pencil does not

drop, such wiry hair
labels that man *black*,
and as he rises, out of his head
flies any small green idea of crop
or the larger one of shop
while the man in the polished shoes
beckons the next body to come,
receive a name at his feet.

A Southern Retrospective:
Portraits from a Private Collection

At the beginning, no oaks or levees
rise behind a river boat.
There is "Henry Durrell III," done up

and framed for 1710. In white knee breeches,
he struts about the South, with a falcon
on his fist and a black boy at his feet

whose white-eyed worshipful look
is a paradigm—he's the first black slave
painted in America, and perhaps that's the reason

why Henry and his falcon were kept on,
framed for the next century, for a time
when the Civil War was not quite ready

for canvas. Its roots were still sunk
in the cotton field when somebody got busy
painting "The Breakdown," dance of a grinning

black boy, red harmonica honking to his feet.
He must be looking forward to "Sunrise
at Fort Sumter, 1864," hung to the right

of "Portrait of a Gentleman," subject unknown.
He has that saintly, anonymous look
coming from too many benedictions with wine.

But it's almost evening in his South
and the gentleman seems comfortably
at home—before home disappeared

and the South gave up those cabins
of happy dancing feet that it had
a hard time painting into place.

Screen Porch

Cicadas bear down with a slow,
rainy song. They draw me
like a nomad tracking fresh weather.
I walk the dusty porch, breathing
ninety degrees of rain
blowing through the canebrake.
Inside, medallioned chandeliers
and cornices of shepherds
offer only cool embroidery
on the hummings of a hot season.
Ceilings rise, vent to skylights,
as if starlight were an answer
to this summer closet of air.

Sharecropper Saturday Night

The corporate man steps out
from behind his scarecrow
and rows of Silver Queen and Country Gentleman
corn to announce that this summer
he sharecrops with his neighbor,
and that last night his latest
woman tossed her skirt over her head
and pranced off to kiss every next guy,
told him to kiss off as she smacked him
with her mother's old fur piece,
one of those little startled mink faces
whose plastic nose plugged him
in the eye, and so naturally he went for
his gun in the car trunk, yelling
at the security guard that he ought to be
shot, that Sweet Jesus, that woman
fired her skirt up in his face,
and she was his for Saturday night.

Homesteading Spring

This shipwreck of a house
lists, its window frames
angling down into spring.

Smell the earth laid open
for stone cutting,
all here the color of shade

where once panes held a torrent
of faces: young eyes
nearsighted with birds clucking

happy as hens in the lilacs,
and the old peering out
for the first April calf

to slip from its mother,
one more plumbed shadow
laid out on the new world.

"Hands at Eighty"

after a photograph by Ann Noggle

A woman's hands are severed
and shot before darkness
like those the saints loved
to hold out to the night
full of questioning and oath.
Here, one hand holds the whiteness
of her own false teeth while the other
is cupped as loosely as a valley
offering emptiness to a hawk.
Still, these hands tingle for attachment—
time, their last snag to latch onto
in space.

Eating Soap

Was it lilies or mother
basted in perfume? Or
was it purer scent
I cupped, wanting
to taste one whole
sweet side of the world?

I went for it
like a swimmer grasping
slick jetty rocks at sea—
washing in, then out,
an underworld saying
just try and hold me.

Immaculate in water,
I rolled flowery lard on my tongue,
my summer dish at three,
thick with lilies
and the aftertaste of Eden.

Sawdust

You made it our home—
the fishpond you built with my mother,

fish flashing from the mossy depths
like chinks of panned gold;

the homemade cherry-bounce,
that bottled wine of October

you set out on the pantry windowsill
each year. Outside, in the musty garage

where woodchips sprinkled from your saw,
stood the three-by-five red tool chest

filled with scrap mahogany. To the end,
it was stamped with my father the sea captain's

name. You never saw his note—
how from his own fish pools, thirty years

removed, he thought of her as she was dying
and wrote his good-bye, a good-bye that she hid

and I found, her a week dead.
Sorting her pale underthings,

I came upon his words, each a flashing
whiteness from that old mirage, the sea.

Four

Cracking Eggs

Once, an orange cat
was so mixed up with the world
there was little room
for here, there, or wherefore-art-thou.

She assumed the claw-tooth rip in the sunset
from a branch in the apple tree,
and at dawn she pooled with light
on the pale pine floor.

She was that brief crack
when the world is perfect blend—
celebration of cat, bird, and shrub—
before things jaggedly go their way.

Strange Music

Mornings in the coffee shop,
you lift the pale cup with your hand,
sounds rattling in your throat
like the gutturals of strutting pigeons.

You never speak. You've never spoken
to me. The moist cakes slip down
in single swallows. You make strange
music and look at me as if I were

nothing, or everything. I watch
your hands rise and you become
implicated. Are you the shape
I was taught, the one under the streetlight

with luminous after-dark hands
and words like licorice twists?
For you could fit the picture
of one closer to home—that shadow

man, with hands rising out of shadow
who came to breathe in my head
when I was ten. Perhaps, you are
the one in the green Ford that stole

my friend away. I dreamed of her
pushing your silvered car-door handle
down and tumbling down a grassy slope
while you sped away. By daylight

she was gone two weeks. Then
she was back in silence.

Everyone said silence
was best.

Poor, large, wordless man,
I have saved my friend from one like you
in dozens of darks, and still I meet
you on corners. You divide.

Standing Wet and Close

Clouds gather. The sheep two-step
this way and that, heat rising
in puffs from their cold lips.
We are like them in our need.
Their soft bodies press
                        while the eyes
remain aloof. Are such expressions
hopeless, and what of the lamb-bleats
that want to be smoothed
even as they are trucked away?
We pause, step closer in the hushed field,
moved by that empty nursery sound.
It's as though the air were waiting,
trying to reknit.
                        Last spring two
hundred huddled like a shepherd's dream
as lightning forked from fleece
to fleece, each sheep stitched
and joined to a single yellow bolt.

Bach in Sumatra: 1944

If that Japanese stockade were to come back
to them, it would come from the rubber forests
where the world divided roughly
into men to the right,
women and children to the left.
Then the rains lined up with bamboo,
and time slowed.

Or perhaps, it persisted in one woman
scoring Bach on orange crates all night,
voices she'd teach in four parts
to women in the dark. By day
there was no variation—a book,
the one book, read over and over to children
who beat each other with sticks
imagining endless war. The text
did not change, and the bodies
never fit the small, thoughtless coffins.

Only the graves opened with room,
past trees, beyond the woman
who started slowly with her prison mates,
making them open their mouths and sing,
fugues rising like Bach, believed-in.

Picturing the Landscape:
"The Grand Teton Block"

In this time frame, a picture frame,
the story stops with winter,
the photographer thrusting his own

wristwatched arm and ruler up to the mountains
like a god measuring out creation.
His shadow cuts across an open geological text—

paragraphs explaining profiles graphing
elegances like Glacier Gulch. In the background
the Tetons themselves loom, rock-rugged

in black and white. Picture them
ranging beyond this *block* in a land-parcel
called Wyoming, out of reach

of this mimicry on the page
and threat of a grade-school ruler.

In the First Place

Moonrise in the Honey Island Swamp,
moon over the wild boar and alligator eyes,
light on the swamp cypress rising from the mist
like creatures on their last, thick legs,
and off to the south there's a city
on marshland, ringed by the grunts
and bellows of a summer night.

*

On the coastal flats, where the river's been
diverted, the engineers blame renegade
pigs that snozzle down to chew the marshgrass roots.
They point fingers at these pink destroyers
of the wetlands who must breathe easy
in the sea air after a long traipse
down from the farm—until the guns go off,
and they're laid out in the moonlit mud.

*

On a 4-H Sunday, it's judgment day,
and Maryanne's pig is lying down in the ring,
groveling in the fresh hay, his competitors
prancing mannerly circles around him.
Maryanne hooks him one with her shepherd's crook,
and he rolls over like a Sunday drunk,
hay drooping from his snout while the crowd cheers
the first-place swine headed out with
his prize of a Smithfield ham.

Three-Year-Old Praising
Mushrooms after Rain

Your hands applaud
this umbrella world,
your breath catching on another day's
discovery: over these wild toadstools you peer
like a navigator struck with the suddenness
of land, its vegetable crest
blooming from the shallows.

Bypass

Near the Fort Payne stockyard
sits a shack,
the kind Walker Evans made the South
sorry for with its baked tar paper
and collard patch, its tobacco tuft
nailed to the porch on this drizzly
day before Thanksgiving. The cattle
bellow malcontent, their concrete pen
sprayed red with inspiration:
Jo w/melaine 4-ever.
The fig tree stands strung to radiance
with pie pans while Jo w/ melaine
inscribe a shortcut
through the background of Thanksgiving.

The Palm Sunday Race

At the barricades we collect, the cathedral's
high clock tolling our start, a hoard
fired forward by the cannon,
sent winding
past the bald priest in his stone
alcove as he waves us on under the sign
for $3 ROOMS blowing purple-lettered
from the India Hotel, and on we pant
past the woman kicking the gas station's
locked bathroom door, roaring FUCK
at the sun as we press into the park,
its live oaks, their branches scraping
the asylum window reinforced with chicken wire
where a boy holds up his drawing of a child
saying HI in green. He waves from his wire
cage and we breathe hard as any mob
flourishing palms on a holy day.

Evolution in the South Bronx

(after an on-site filming of a horror movie made for TV)

Telephone directories still open in the wind
to the right page, the right name
where no one is at home. Or will be.
Room by room they've left the streets
with the staunch Dutch names.

It's no longer a matter of the lady-of-the-house,
off doing a night cleaning job in pine oil,
being out. There's no one left
to wait for the last bus
slowing in the rain.

Even crime's moved out.
No one knows the difference
between the windy stacks of hallways
and alleys in moonlight. And tonight,
it's all a horror movie set:

floodlights capture a pack of men
turned wolves—such an exotic setting
for a night of family TV, the furred men
embarking on a screenful of entrails
while the homeviewers fiddle at the table

with remains on their Blue Delft dinner plates.
The wolves have made it
past Jack London and his campfires;
they're capitalizing on the Bronx,
they're in the dining room.

The Radio Says Buy

yourself a star for Christmas.
No need to look one green inch
further—for $35 we will send
certified coordinates of where
to find yourself. You can be
that star named Sue. It's your inextinguishable
right to own a gift that lasts.

Remember our president saluting
the dead Marines who he said
were guarding the gates to heaven?
Now we can all be there at their elbows,
shining down on what's left
of forever.

Still Life with Grass, Fur, and Air at the Museum of Natural History

Between the surfacing blue whale and Hope
diamond, there's a hallway of suns
and small arrested hearts.

Deep in this corridor, I watch
flared nostrils drained of forest breath,
and mountains in flattened panorama

behind this figment of a caribou. He stands
so quiet and elegant, full of summer
grass, but with such an easy eye

turned away from the plain.

Rembrandt's Vanities

I

318 years and 14,000 square feet
of flagstone later, the town fathers

are using the self-portraits to identify
your bones mixed into the pauper pit

beneath Amsterdam's Western Church.
Vain little trick you played though,

painting yourself enough beauty
to die behind, enough perfection

to confound a whole line of computers
busily designing you a skull. You,

who coated yourself with hues of apricot
and plum in the fur-dark rooms, go on

vanishing. Lie quiet among those
never born for limelight,

those born to disappear
into history's stone-gray privacy.

II

Today it's enigma they encounter
in the painting's darkly paired eyes—

the anatomical technicians up against
the crystal ball of an imagination

swirled around the skull. So
they study bones beneath the flagstone

for a possible Rembrandt, seeking
revelation from signs of ingested lead.

Does one of them picture you chewing
a raisin cake, pondering

above the oily glaze of colors—
these men who pick through a dark

of pelvic bones looking for sex,
looking for the right son of a miller?

III

Where lies the skull of the right son
of the right miller? The one that thought

in amber, then purple tint. There's not
one scar or palsied eye to mar his painted

flesh—poor dead beauty makes a mock
of us. Rembrandt, unhonorable man,

makes a mock of our century
turned toward an end.

Summer Tomatoes

The blind woman's face shows no puzzles
the sunlight makes. She passes
as through a clearing while all around
the summer softens on windowsills,
tomatoes shading from green
to heavy red, and here by the roadside
two dead kittens curl
like small sisters tossed from the night,
these furs and skins, our own
slow measuring of ends.

Twins

All morning I watch the spring sun
fall on a fresh altar of birch.
Now, by the rowhouses, dark apartments
stack out of the alders, and the light
keeps pouring down.

In the dirt road, a girl stands
by her blue bike, nodding up at
two small golden heads lodged in the May air:
heads, shoulders, and four wiggling hands
pinned by a fallen window.

The two loud sisters yell at each other,
then at the blue-biked girl,
then at me,
their world shut down
to our little trinity.

As I rattle the wobbly doorknob,
they hush in their spring stock,
listening. We wait on the verge
of a season holding
saviors and the saved.

Listen

As a child that January you knew
it was not the place to be:
in the cellar-cold, squatting
behind the furnace, your flashlight
stopping on kittens that were tiny
gray curls, on fur that did not
move in and out. And today
you arrive at that place
you've known of since the kittens
covered with ash. Outside,

January blows, and inside,
you lie cold on a table
under a sheet, the doctor's sonorphone
pressing your pelvis for something
not in *Gray's Anatomy* high on the shelf.
Everyone is silent, watching
blips on a computer screen, as you hear
yourself say *my bladder's so full
I could die*. You catch those words
like a first hard slap. It is January
now. It was January then
behind the furnace.
Listen.

Short Street

Vapo-Rub is blowing through
my dream, through that green, wooden house,
corner of Fern and Short.
Your Granny is taking her time
dying again, and I arrive routinely
to sit on a stretcher parked outside her window.
The phone keeps ringing
while grandaughters, paired to a room,
doze and grow toward perfume.

Tonight, the stretcher is my task.
I welcome its broad, flat emptiness.
Your white-skinned Granny coughs
at a cat from my old marriage
scratching her window screen.
Wobbly-fleeced and dying
it thuds to the flower bed.

In this flux of cats and women
shrunk to grandmothers,
my own dead mother arrives,
her forehead calcified to dust.
All the way from Short Street,
they've come to converge like youth
laid out cold in midair.

October

Little brown dog, gone fishing,
paw-deep in autumn sky of the creek—
the minnows are around him,
they tempt like deer flagging
white-tailed through the field.

> For one slow rainy season
> I was made quiet by your body,
> its thickening summer stalk—
> desire and need a tangled beginning.

The dog peers past his own toothiness
quivering on the stream's light.
His minnows are traveling away.
In and out, and away. A tongue-lap away.

> That day you looked at me looking
> into you like space under the wet gold
> leaves, the message was about leaving.
> It echoed and left us with closed eyes.

Why do surfaces hold the face
aloft, while minnows swirl truantly
beneath? We're no more than ripply smiles
stretched across the depths.

> Why take your head from my belly?
> Let's turn desire loose,
> or shall we turn it to need,
> make it a cold and twisted thing?
> Bulls cleave to the hillside
> with a bellowing for this.

Waterstriders play stretch
on the surface but tonight
this glass-bottomed-boat-

of-a-creek will hold the stars,
a sparkle long gone as it's seen.

> Under my footsteps, one day,
> twigs snapped, and eight wild turkeys
> gusted with fear from the trees,
> beauty and need set off. I want you
> to hear through my skin.

Quiet, staring water-dog,
these minnows are not trees
to run to, and you can't eat
this wet covering of sunlight.
It fascinates—the dare
of disappearance behind every move.

About the Author

Katherine Soniat's first collection of poems won the Camden Poetry Prize (1985), and she was second place winner of the 1989 Virginia Prize for Poetry. Her work has appeared in many journals such as *Poetry, The Yale Review, The Ohio Review, The Kenyon Review, The Antioch Review, The North American Review,* and *The Nation.* She teaches at Hollins College and lives in Catawba, Virginia.

80